message-door
весть-дверь

*An Anthology of Contemporary
Surrealist Poetry from Russia*

Edited and translated by Anatoly Kudryavitsky

SV
SurVision Books

First published in 2020 by
SurVision Books
Dublin, Ireland
www.survisionmagazine.com

Introduction © Anatoly Kudryavitsky, 2020
English translations © Anatoly Kudryavitsky, 2006, 2018, 2020
Original Russian-language poems © their individual authors, 2020
This collection copyright © SurVision Books, 2020
Design © SurVision Books, 2020

ISBN: 978-1-912963-17-1

Acknowledgements

Grateful acknowledgement is made to the editors of the following, in
which a number of these translations, or versions of them, originally
appeared:

Aus deinem Auge schlüpft der Kuckuck (Lychatz Verlag, Leipzig, 2017),
Cyphers, Mirror Sand anthology (Glagoslav Publications, 2018), *A
Night in the Nabokov Hotel* anthology (Dedalus Press, 2006), *Plume,
Poetry Ireland Review, The SHOp, Shot Glass Journal, SurVision,
Transformations* by Sergey Biryukov (SurVision Books, 2018), *World
Poetry Almanac* (Ulaanbaatar, Mongolia).

Some of these poems, in English translation, were first broadcast on
RTÉ Radio 1.

Introduction

It is a common knowledge that there weren't any Surrealist poetic groups in Russia, however quite a number of artists, poets and fiction writers appreciated artistic ideas of the Surrealists and followed them in their work. The aesthetics of such Russian futurist poets as Alexey Kruchenykh, Igor Terentyev, Velimir Khlebnikov, David Burliuk, Olga Rozanova, and Ilya Zdanevich is rather comparable to that of Dada and Surrealism. The same goes for the Paris-based émigré Boris Poplavsky, one of the finest poets in the Russian language. The German poet Hugo Ball, the founder of the Dada movement, was friendly with Kandinsky; they spent quite some time discussing poetic experiments of the Russian futurists, and so participated in an exchange of "poetic air".

After the last World War, Evgeny Kropivnitsky, Genrikh Sapgir and Igor Kholin were the most prominent among the Moscow writers that came to be associated with the now well-known Lianozovo group. These poets had a Dostoyevskian eye for the grotesque and often surreal aspects of everyday Russian life, which made their work immediately accessible. Strictly speaking, these poets were not Surrealists, but their verse sounded fresh and enriched the Russian language to a great extent. Gennady Aigi (1934–2006), a prominent Russian and Chuvash poet, created his own language, an independent and unique speech or, if you prefer, chant. His poems are derived entirely from individual words and sometimes from single syllables and sounds. In each of his works, he gave birth to some kind of a parallel, surreal *universum*.

All the afore-mentioned poets paved the way for modern-days Russian Surrealism.

Behind Sergey Biryukov born in the South of Russia and currently living in Germany, stand the famous Russian Futurist poets. He published a couple of monographs about Russian *avant-garde* and *zaum* poetry. Biryukov is prone to experiment with syntax and language rather than with the available voices, and so is the younger-generation poet, Sergey Tenyatnikov currently based in Spain. Tenyatnikov excels in creating surreal parables; he is one of the two bilingual poems included in this book; his other language is German, whereas the editor of this book is also an English-language Surrealist poet.

Tatyana Grauz inhabits approximately the same territory as Aigi. Her poems seemingly exist outside time, where each of them creates a sound image; often a surreal one. Her style can be defined as minimalism. She often focuses her attention on individual words or even on fragments of those words and sound units from them.

Dmitri Grigoriev of St. Petersburg and Anna Glazova, who used to live and teach in the USA and currently lives in Germany, often portray urban blight and paranoia. Grigoriev's work can be best described as that of a magic realist capable of generating a fictitious world and populating it with surreal elements. One can trace the sources of Anna Glazova's minimalist texts to early Surrealist and even Zen poetry, and it definitely displays parallels to the visual arts.

Yuri Milorava born in Georgia but now living in Moscow and the young Moscow poet Sasha Moroz demonstrate more typical surrealist approaches to poetry writing, seemingly following Andre Breton's postulates. They both are minimalists, too, and they build their poems from some snippets of reality often interlaced with dream sequences; they explore the possibilities of silence bonding parts of their poems to each other and making them stand up as such.

This book offers an opportunity to hear a few new voices in Russian poetry. These poets are destined to shape the Russian poetry of the future. What they have achieved is considerable but they all, especially the younger-generation poets, have a great leap forward in them.

Anatoly Kudryavitsky
Dublin, Ireland

Сергей Бирюков

В сторону знака

Jerzy Faryno

узнать как пятятся корни
деревьев
в сторону знака
в сторону корня из минус единицы
понять обратный ход
это собственно вот
постижение
на уровне меты и мета
и движение
от к до
и обратное
обратное знака
(запомнить)

Towards a Sign

For Jerzy Faryno

To find out about the roots of trees
how they move backward
toward a sign
toward the square root of minus one
to comprehend that backward movement
this is what I call
an insight
at the sign level, at the meta level
and a movement
from some spot to another
and back
is the reverse of a sign
(something to remember)

В доме Магритта

Филипу Меерсману

улитка впилась в чрево Олимпии
вечность и невозможность
трансперсональность
но
завиток боли Жоржет
Ренэ Магритт пишет на кухне
вскипает кофе
трубка сопит
человек без лица
изображает шкаф
легкое перевоплощение
вещного мира
еще секунда
и улица
пустится
вдогонку

In Magritte's House

For Philip Meersman

The snail sank into Clympia's womb
eternity and impossibility
transpersonality
but
the curl of Georgette's pain
René Magritte writes in the kitchen
the coffee boils
the pipe whizzes
the faceless man
impersonates a wardrobe
The world of things
its effortless reincarnation
A few more seconds –
and the street
will dash
after it

* * *

полцарства отдают
и метят лепетом
сплетают голени
над речкой
вот ведь что
жизнь
не начнется заново
поэтому
остановись мгновение
постой

прохожий молвит
битте где дорога к фаусту
ви ланге дауерт
вся эта кутерьма

я проходил когда-то
ну так запросто
и не смотрел
на стертые дома

но дальше что
но дальше что
но дальше

Towards Faust

They give away half the kingdom
having marked it with some prattle
their legs interlaced
over the river
so that's what it is
your life
won't begin anew
hence
"Beautiful moment,
do not pass away!"

a passer-by says
bitte could you show me the way to Faust?
wie lange dauert
this commotion?

I once passed here
casually
without looking
at the erased houses

but now what
but where do we go from here
but on we go

Продолжение сна

невозможно запомнить но все-таки
хотя бы в обрывках
запоминается продолжение
сна
почему-то неизвестное место
что-то вроде классной комнаты
где рюкзаки и сумки свалены
брошены кое-как
несколько знакомых лиц
но неточно определяемых
то ли он то ли похожий на
она или похожая на нее
словно ты приехал неизвестно
откуда приехала она неизвестно
полный неясностей и недомолвок
разговор
огоньки сигарет щелканье зажигалок
обратная последовательность действий
ты отвечаешь предвидя вопрос
почесываешь переносицу
после получения известий
собственно нет даже слов
ну так полусловья
фрагменты речи
опустошение
продолжение сна
видимость бесконеч

A Dream Continued

It's impossible to remember but still
—at least in scraps—
you can memorise the continuation
of a dream
some unknown place
looking like a classroom
bags and backpacks dumped
all over the floor
a few familiar faces
though inaccurately outlined
is he really or does he only resemble
is she or isn't she
as if you've returned from Goodness knows
where or she's come back from nothingness
a conversation
full of omissions and ambiguities
glowing cigarettes the clicks of lighters
the reverse sequence of events
you answer a predicted question
scratch your nose
having learned the news
actually words are missing too
only half-words are left
fragments of speech
devastation
a continuation of a dream
a semblance of infini...

* * *

вы так же встаете
из кроватей
из могил
зверочеловеки
набираете еды
из животных
растений
и уносите
в могилу
Только надпись
настоящие растворены
в пространстве
или времени
над ними
нет плиты
нет

Beastmen

In the same old way
you get out of your beds
of your graves
—beastmen—
gather some food
rodents
vegetables
and take it all
back to your crypts

Inscriptions: signboards...
the genuine ones
dissolved in space
or in time
no tombstones
on their graves
none whatsoever

Анна Глазова

* * *

иногда так ложится
рука между лопаток
что сквозь них
вдруг открывается
яма в небо;

туда можно было бы провалиться и лечь

если бы небо
не означало:
отсутствие дна.

Anna Glazova

Heaven

sometimes a hand
lands between the shoulder blades
and all of a sudden they
disclose
a hole into the sky;

one could fall into it and lie down there

if heaven
didn't signify
the lack of a bottom.

* * *

смена состояний
со скоростью ночного падения.

сроки со свистом вносятся в сроки,
подбирать их ходит
случай,
зверь времеяд,
зубы — прямо из дна
сводного дня.

Time Frame

a change of state
at the speed of a night fall.

deadlines enter other deadlines with a swish
an accident walks around
and gathers them,
the beast called timeeater,
its teeth come straight from the bottom
of a consolidated day.

А. Ф.

слова тоже звери
но живут в сторону прошлого
и за ними идёшь не вперёд
а по следу

темноту раздвигая руками
и сбиваясь на шёпот.

только сами они
расставляют ловушки
а когда попадёшься —
зовут жалобно
не по имени.

For A. F.

words too are wild beasts
but they live towards the past
so there's no point in going after them
you just follow in their tracks

parting darkness with your hands
and switching to a whisper.

the only thing, they too
set traps
and if you get caught,
they call out for you dolefully
but never by your name.

* * *

пар от чтения
поднимается в губы читателю.
оседает на коже
запах кожи писавшего.

буква ещё выдыхается.

прикоснись — если чувствуешь тягу,
тебя увлекло.

Reading

the reading steam
rises up to a reader's lips,
accumulates on his skin.
the writer's skin smell.

the letter keeps losing its fragrance.

touch it – if you feel the pull
you've been carried away.

* * *

зеркало тёмного вида
которого нет.
и не смотри куда всё оно катится.

но и на свет не смотри,
ничего твой глаз не обнимет.

взглядом измерить от травы и до кроны —
настоящий объём человека.

Vision

a darkview mirror
that doesn't exist.
don't check where all things roll to.

don't look at the light either,
your sight will embrace nothing.

to measure visually – from the grass to the crown –
the real height of a man.

Татьяна Грауз

Утренний сон

ночью в разрушенном доме
кто-то стучался в закрытую дверь
кто-то входил в опустевшие комнаты
жёлтые листья — капли увядшего света
по подоконнику шелестели тревожно

Morning Dream

at night someone was knocking
at the closed door of a ruined house
someone entered the empty rooms
yellow leaves—drops of withered light—
rustled uneasily on the windowsill

* * *

в свете июля зелень паслёна
     х р у с т а л ь н а
нужно ль ещё что-нибудь?
может быть отсвет дрожащий
     зелёный
в воде голубой?

July's Light

in July's light the emerald of the nightshade
        crystal clear
do we need anything else?
maybe a shimmering sheen of
        green
in the blue of the water?

* * *

вот и опять
беспричинно улыбчиво небо
   будто после болезни
   будто снят карантин
к реке босиком
в озноб прозрачной воды
не наступить на улиток
осокой ладонь не поранить
   когда вечереет прозрачно
    и небо прозрачно
невозвратимо звенит

The Sky

once again
an unreasonably smiling sky
     as though after an i ness
     as though the quarantine's over
towards the river barefoot
into the chill of the clear water
avoiding stepping on snails
escaping sedge-leaf hand cuts
     when the decline of the say is transparent
       and the sky is transparent
and rings irrevocably

Неяркое солнце

в одноразовом дне неделимо
        сияние сада
        холодок синевы
и боярышника багровые пятна
            и неяркое солнце
        и дождь переменный

такая казалось бы монотонная жизнь
    такие скупые подробности
            будто перед разлукой
разглядывает припоминая душа

Soft Sun

Inside a disposable day they are indivisible:
       the shining of the garden
     the chilly blueness
the crimson stains of the hawthorn
        the soft sun
    and the fickle rain

such a seemingly monotonous life
  so few details
     as though the soul before departure
scrutinises them trying to remember

Апрель-голубка

проточный свет
        день чистопрудный
апрель-голубка в теплынь недремлющего неба
     на льдинке солнца незаметно проплывает
как мы быть может
        может быть когда-то

April-Dove

flowing light
              the clear-pond day
April-Dove in the warmth of the watchful sky
       floating by insensibly on a little
              ice flow of the Sun
as we will perhaps
              perhaps one day

Дмитрий Григорьев

* * *

Во тьме ты светишься...
Ночные мотыльки
стучатся в твою кожу,
на крыльях каждого —
мои глаза...
А я перебираю буквы,
похожие на яблочные зерна,
и слова не могу сказать...

Dmitry Grigoriev

Night

In the darkness, your shining...
Night moths
tap on your skin;
each wing
shows my eyes.
I leaf through letters
that resemble apple seeds,
but no words find a way out...

* * *

Положи мои слова на землю,
утрамбуй их ногами, чтобы не поднимались,
чтобы сеточка подошвы отпечаталась на каждом,
чтобы никто их не трогал и,
проходя мимо, каждый говорил: «Бросовая вещь».
Чтобы их засыпало снегом,
чтобы на них мочились собаки,
чтобы они были незаметны словно
прошлогодние листья,
чтобы, глядя на них,
говорили: «Земля…»

Тогда подними мои слова к небу.

Words

Lay my words on the ground,
tread them down, ram them firmly,
so that the pattern of the sole leaves a mark on them,
and no one ever touches them,
and each passer-by mutters: "Such a useless thing" –
and snow covers them,
dogs urinate on them,
and they become indistinguishable
like rotten leaves,
and people, looking at them, say:
"That's clay."

Then raise them up to the sky.

* * *

Ночью:
серые мотыльки прячутся
в складках моей одежды.
Они наполняют мой костюм,
шелест их крыльев похож
на мой шепот.
А когда на улице
зажигают фонари,
они вместе летят на свет,
и костюм движется,
словно это я иду, скрывая лицо
под глубоко надвинутой шапкой,
но мои глаза – лишь рисунок на крыльях,
и душа моя – пыль.

Shades of Night

At night
grey moths hide themselves
in secret folds of my clothes.
They fill my suit.
Rustling of their wings sounds like
my whisper.

When all the street lamps
begin to shine
the moths fly up to them –
and my suit seems to be moving
as though I walk hiding my face,
my hat pulled over my eyes.

Ah, my eyes are circles on butterflies' wings,
and my soul is dust.

* * *

Мне говорили:
Полезные вещи нельзя на помойку,
полезные вещи еще пригодятся.
Мне подарили большую коробку:
в эту коробку поместится много
полезных вещей.
Мне нравится эта коробка,
она стоит улыбаясь,
в ней очень тепло и уютно
и я в ней легко умещаюсь,
а значит, я очень полезен
и, значит, еще пригожусь.

Not Rubbish

They used to say,
Don't scrap good things,
they will come in handy.
They presented me with a cardboard box
big enough to store
loads of good things in it...

I have a liking for this box
that stands here smiling.
It is big enough to accommodate me.
I feel cosy in it, I am warm.

Maybe this means that I am a good thing
and will come in handy.

* * *

Рыбак ищет червей в навозной куче
но находит алмазы их уже целая груда
– Разве рыба клюет на алмазы,
и откуда здесь эти
сверкающие семена
прошедшие сквозь тела животных?
– Пастух должно быть влюбился, –
– ему сосед отвечает, –
– и стадо паслось в небесах.

Diamonds

A fisherman searches for worms in a dunghill
but finds diamonds, a whole pile of them.
Can diamonds be fish bait? he asks himself.
Where do these sparkling seeds
come from and how did they pass
through the animals' bodies?
His neighbour replies:
The shepherd must have fallen in love,
so the herd grazed in heaven.

Анатолий Кудрявицкий

El corazón

Сердце
кальмар в костной клетке

Радуйся, могучий планктон!

Он пришел ко мне с пузырьком чернил
он спрашивал о смерти
его часы танцевали жигу

Море подтягивает кожу
сердца пульсируют случайностью

Эти берега не обоймут время

Небо прикрывает свой неон
бледными пальцами

Anatoly Kudryavitsky

El corazón

Human heart
a squid in a bony cage

Rejoice, you mighty plankton!

He came to me with a bubble of ink
he inquired about death
   his watch dancing a gigue

The sea pulls its skin
hearts pulsate for changes

These shores will never contain time

The sky covers its neon
   with its pale fingers

Камень

Прикоснись к обращенному в камень
силуэты сидящих в кругу
их свечные глаза
прикоснись к своему прикосновению

Тихие вихри сущности
капли малинового и морского
соки гнева, испуганные кораллы
Что было моим, отломлено

У каждого имени есть тело
сапфировые воры, их огненная одежда
соборы, архитектура умов
Заметь стыдливость самоидентификации

Жалость никогда не возвращается
Попробуй на вкус гранулы хаоса
Тетраэдры твоих возрастов
уходят в сумерки

Как все это превращается в камень

Stone

Touch things turned to stone
silhouettes sitting in a circle
their candle eyes
touch your touch

Silent whirlwinds of essence
droplets of crimson and marine blue
juices of anger, panicking corals
What was mine is now detached

Every name has a body
sapphire thieves wear fire
cathedrals, the architecture of a mind
Mark the identity blush

Pity never comes back
Taste these granules of havoc
Tetrahedrons of your ages
walk into your walk

How it all turns to stone

Бард-декламатор

Где-то в углу языка...
Джули Фландерс

Запах непрочитанных полей... Вечность
слаба на слух
Мусорные баржи идеологии
засыпают наши уши

Преданность выживает как сердце
Кедровый коричневый лед
триангуляция Как позвонить
ближайшей стяжке времен?

Наша жизнь — ежедневные похороны
паника атомов У языка
много углов
с разбрызганным птичьим светом

Твой снежный запах мертвое тепло
твоего тела... немощный старик
с мешком повестей
под круглой книгой луны

Reacaire

Somewhere in the corner of language...
—Julie Flanders

The scent of unread fields... Eternity
is hard of hearing.
Trash barges of an ideology
earth up our ears.

Our allegiances surv ve as hearts.
Brown ice of cedars. Triangulation.
What's the lo-call number
for the nearest time stretch?

We live the daily funeral,
the panic of atoms. Language
has many corners
sprinkled with birds' early light.

Your snow perfume, the dead warmth
of your body... A sick man
with his sack of stories
under the round book of the moon.

Reacaire: reciter of poems (Irish Gaelic)

53

Реканати

Опера – мечта плотника
оперы рождаются без речи
оковрованными

Из керамического рта
облачко утр
два каменных ангела
в дверях
смесь сознания и тела

Дай мне дымного леопарда
окружи гвардией гардений

пусть расплывается желтизна

Каменные плиты здороваются с подошвами
монастырская лестница дышит
изгнанием

Голос, шаг –
один из них слеп

Recanati

Opera is a carpenter's dream
operas are born carpeted
and speechless

A cloudlet of mornings
out of the ceramic mouth
two cracked stone angels
coddling the doors
a mixture of consciousness and body

Bring me a smoke leopard
place me among guarded gardenias

let the yellowness expand

Stone slabs recognise the feet
the monastic staircase exhales
exile

The voice, the pace—
one of them blind

Мотив для терменвокса

Модильяни не умер
ваяет в Африке
пальцы вылепили множество голов
что говорят одновременно

Бог превозносит простоту
хоть вселенная меняет очертания
с каждым его вдохом
Его ультразвуковое пение тревожит
его поклонниц, коноплянок

A Tune for Theremin Vox

Modigliani is not dead
he is sculpting in Africa
His fingers have shaped numerous heads
that all talk at the same time

God praises simplicity
although the Universe changes shape
with every breath he takes
His ultrasound singing disturbs
his worshippers, the linnets

Юрий Милорава

* * *

единый
грубый дом на гребне
сожженья слой
из дыма
движущегося
несоразмерно

Untitled 1

a single
rugged house on the ridge
a burned layer shows
through the smoke
that moves
disproportionately

* * *

шоссе
со штабелями расколотых
не омытых
как малые дети в юдоли
и искореженных
глобальных
ликов

Untitled 2

a motorway
with stacks of cracked
unwashed
—like small children in the vale—
and twisted
global
faces

* * *

тайный винт
как розовая губчатость
цветы
внизу
повороты
шум
буйволы у воды
след угля и соли
множество стеклянных колонн

Untitled 3

a secret screw
like pink sponginess
flowers
down below
turns of the road
noise
buffaloes by the water
a trail of coal and salt
a multitude of glass columns

* * *

ввинчена
сдвинута
в монограмме упрека
в шуме
потаенная
весть-дверь

Untitled 4

screwed in
shifted
inside the monogram of reproach
amid the noise
a concealed
message-door

* * *

зеленые легкие
или землистые
текут
ступени травами
вниз место теней
и пустот
ком
прозрачный

Untitled 5

the steps
green weightless
or earth-coloured
flow in a grass-like way
down to the place of shadows
and gaps
a transparent
clod

Саша Мороз

коллекция

нецелые части всегда заменяют чужие кости:
коровьи позвонки, берцовые кости оленей над ванной,
куриные косточки у собаки,
зубы, челюсти, ногти, волосяные кулоны, слоновые серьги.
влажный воздух вокруг камней, травы, бумаг, слов

ловля ангелов напоминает весеннюю ловлю сусликов

деревянные глазки окружают ребенка во время сна.
говори со мной
словно закатываешь баночку с огурцами
некоторые части непременно выпадают из числа костей и
    образуют полости

collection

non-integral bits always replace other bones:
cow vertebrae, deer tibia over the bathtub,
dogs' chicken bones,
teeth, jaws, nails, hair pendants, ivory earrings.
humid air around stones, grass, paper, words

catching angels is like gopher hunting in spring

wooden eyes encircle a baby as it sleeps.
talk to me
the way you pickle cucumbers
some bits always get omitted from bones and form cavities

* * *

вода начинает искать
как звали того, кто пошел на аллею
скоро-приёмники
женщины
серый оранжевый галстук
музей лошадей
все спят

Untitled 1

water begins to look up the name
of the man who's gone out to the alley
short-term receivers
women
a greyish orange tie
a museum of horses
everyone's asleep

* * *

земля, усеянная
лед, усеянный
согни в коленях
хотелось бы оказаться
бенгальские огни
не превратится в дерево
когда наступит
ортодонт
двадцать московских художников
волосяной апокалипсис
два яйца взбить
один стакан тертой муки круп
два стакана моркови
огонь

Untitled 2

the land dotted with ..
ice, also dotted
bend your knees
I'd like to get to
the sparklers
it won't turn into a tree
when this happens
orthodontist
twenty Moscow artists
the apocalypse of hair
two eggs to whisk
one cup of grated cereals and flour
two cups of carrots
fire

* * *

большое осеннее поле
серия описаний, в которых
большие рыбы
апельсины, лимоны, молотый тмин
самообразовавшиеся объекты
закрашенные зеркала
сонатная форма
упражнение номер один
санный след

Untitled 3

the large autumn field
a series of descriptions in which
there're big fish
oranges, lemons, ground caraway seeds
self-generated objects
painted mirrors
the sonata form
exercise number one
a toboggan track

* * *

рыжая рубашка, снятая с цветка,
чем-то выпачкана.
стыд. глагол, ещё глагол, сон.
мощи над цветком.
хрупкие кости трутся о камень
стон – это цикл. глагол. бык над цветком.
мокрые пряди прилипли к спине,
она стоит задом к волнам.
«кто это – бык?»

Untitled 4

red shirt taken off a flower,
stained.
shame. a verb, another verb, a dream.
relics over the flower.
fragile bones rub against the rock.
groan is a sequence. a verb. a bull over the flower.
she stands with her back facing the waves,
wet tresses stuck to her shoulders.
who's that, a bull?

Улитка на обочине

Алёнке

здесь должны были быть стихи
об улитке, о её жизни в зарослях.
но вместо стихов
я написал детектив:
неизвестный преступник
убил маленькую улитку и выбросил её труп
на обочину дороги. полиция теряется в догадках,
в поисках улик прочёсывает густую траву
мелкой расчёской. прошёл слух о маньяке.
все улитки в округе опасаются покидать дома...
читатель любит детективные истории,
прости, улитка.

Sergey Tenyatnikov

A Snail on the Roadside

For Alenka

this page should have been dedicated to a poem
about a snail, about its life in the thicket.
but instead of poetry
I've written a detective story:
an unidentified criminal killed
a tiny snail and left its corpse
on the roadside. the police are at a loss,
they search for clues, they comb the thick grass
with a fine-tooth comb. There's a rumour going around
about a serial killer. all the local snails are wary of leaving home...
readers love crime fiction;
sorry, little snail.

Памяти П. Д. З.

не верь никому: ни веку, ни внуку.
из ветки растут твои уши,
из ветра растут твои губы.
там, где ты плывёшь,
воде не нужен стакан,
там, где ты живёшь,
из твоего глаза вылупляется кукушка.
не верь никому, что сумма
сошедшей с ума материи — мертва.
ты сам теперь — распаханная земля:
в тебе больше правды,
чем во всех словах,
в тебе больше надежды,
чем во всех делах.

In memory of P. D. Z.

don't trust anyone: neither the century nor your grandson.
your ears grow from a branch,
your lips from the wind.
at the point you're swimming to
water doesn't need a glass;
at the point where you're living
a cuckoo hatches from your eye.
don't trust anyone who is saying
the whole mad matter is dead.
you are the plowed and now:
there's more truth in you
than in all the words,
more hope in you
than in all the goings-on.

Неизбранное произведение

как держит земля людей...
истоптанная живыми,
вымощенная мёртвыми,
исписанная цитатами
улиц и прозой ландшафта.

как держит полка книги...
потрёпанные переплёты,
плесень, пепел, пыль.
и как полка без книг — земля
без людей такая же плоская.

An Uncollected Poem

how the soil holds people...
trodden by the living,
paved with dead bodies,
inscribed with quotations of the
streets and the fiction of landscapes.

how a shelf holds books...
tattered bindings,
mould, ashes, dust.
and, like a bookless shelf, the humanless earth
remains flat.

В кастрюле булькает время

в кастрюле булькает время,
в пальцах щёлкает кремень.
пахнет палённым волосом,
слушаю собственный голос.
мне ненавистно истории
эпическое старение –
её писк самки комара
над лысиной Гомера.

Time in the Pan

Time is bubbling in the pan,
fingers click like flints.
it smells of burning hair.
I listen to my voice.
I hate the epic ageing
of history, the way it lets out
a female-mosquito squeak
over the bald head of Homer.

Послежитие

После того как меня убили, я поднялся на небо и приземлился на облаке Семь. Мой отец подошёл ко мне и обнял меня. Он налил мне водки. Мы выпили. Я посмотрел на Землю. Она была похожа на одноклеточный организм. Отец спросил меня, как поживают люди и доступны ли им плоды дерева познания. Я ответил, что у людей — как всегда — всё хорошо и что плоды дерева познания я никогда не видел в свободной продаже. Зато даже зимой есть свежая клубника и бананы. Мы выпили ещё пару рюмок. Стемнело, и отец ушёл спать. Я уселся на облаке поудобнее, достал микроскоп и стал разглядывать Землю: грязные, бородатые мужчины гнались за другими грязными, бородатыми мужчинами. Некоторые из них падали и оставались лежать на Земле.

Afterlife

After being killed, I ascended to heaven and landed on Cloud Seven. My father came up to me and hugged me. He poured me some vodka, and we had a drink. I glanced at the Earth; it resembled a unicellular organism. Father asked me how people were getting on and whether they could easily obtain fruits of the tree of knowledge. I replied by saying that people, as always, were doing well and that I had never seen fruits of the tree of knowledge on sale, however even in winter time one could buy fresh strawberries and bananas. We emptied a couple more glasses. It got dark, and my father retired to bed. I positioned myself comfortably atop the cloud, took out a microscope, and began to examine the Earth. Dirty bearded men were chasing after some other dirty bearded men. A few of them fell and remained lying on the Earth.

Biographical Notes

Sergey Biryukov was born in 1950 in Tambov. He lived in Moscow, and is currently based in Halle, Germany. Having started writing poetry at the end of 1960s, he only saw his first poem published in a literary magazine in 1989. Since then, he has published many collections of his poems; the first of them, *The Muse of Zaum* (1980) and the most recent two, *The Run of Books* and *Calling* (both 2015). He also published the monograph entitled *Zevgma: Russian Poetry, Mannerism to Postmodernism* (1994), as well as a number of books on the history and theoretical aspects of Russian avant-garde. He was the founder and President of the Academy of Zaum, which includes Futurist poets from everywhere in Russia. His work has been translated into several European languages; a book of his poems in English translation, *Transformations,* was published by SurVision Books in 2018. He won first prize at the Berlin International Poetry Competition, and was the recipient of the Alexey Kruchenykh Poetry Award.

Anna Glazova was born in 1973 in Dubna near Moscow. A poet, a literary translator and a critic, she studied in Germany and did postgraduate studies at Northwestern University (Evanston, Illinois). She taught literature at a few universities in the USA, and now is based in Hamburg, Germany. Five collections of her poetry have been published in Russia: *Even if It's Water* (2003), *A Loop. Not Half of It* (2008), *For a Shrew* (2013), *A Dream Experience* (2014) and *Soil Atop the Earth* (2016). She translated into Russian, among others, Paul Celan and Ernest Yandl, and her own poems have been translated into a number of languages. In 2013, she won the Andrei Bely Prize for her collection of poems titled *For a Shrew.*

Tatiana Grauz (pen name of Tatyana Griolooz) was born in Chelyabinsk in 1964. She was educated at the Moscow Medical Academy and at the Russian Academy of Theatre Arts, and worked in Moscow as a theatre director, occasionally appearing on stage and in feature films as an actress. She has published three collections of her textual and visual poems, *Too Much Space* (2004), *More Transparent than the Sky* (2005) and *Forest-Lake-Garden* (2014). Her poems have been translated into English, Swedish, Japanese and Chuvash. She won the David Burliuk Prize for life-long commitment to experimental poetry.

Dmitry Grigoriev was born in 1960 in St. Petersburg, where he still lives. A graduate of Leningrad State University, he travelled the world extensively, and wrote poetry, however he wasn't allowed to publish anything until perestroika. Some of his poems, though, found their way onto the pages of a few American Russian-language magazines. At the beginning of 1990s three collections of his poems appeared in St. Petersburg. He is now regarded as one of the most important St. Petersburg poets of his generation. A volume of his *Selected Unpublished Poems* came out in 1992. Since then, he has published three novels, a book of his short stories, a travel book and seven collections of poetry, including *Crossroads* (1995), *Fiery Yard-Keeper* (2005), *The Other Photographer* (2009) and *New Fairy Tales* (2011).

Anatoly Kudryavitsky was born in 1954 in Moscow, of mixed Polish/Irish parentage. Having lived in Russia and Germany, he has been based in Dublin since the beginning of the century. Educated at Moscow Medical University, he later worked as a researcher in immunology, a journalist, and a literary translator. He has published three novels, a book of short stories, eight collections of his Russian poems, the most recent being *The Book of Gimmicks: Collected Prose Poems* (Evgeny Stepanov Publishing, 2017) and

Outlines (Free Poetry Publishing, 2020), as well as five collections of his English-language poems, the latest being *The Two-Headed Man and the Paper Life* (MadHat Press, USA, 2019). He has edited and translated into English four bilingual anthologies of contemporary German, Ukrainian and Russian poetry published by Dedalus Press (Ireland) and Glagoslav Publications (UK). He won the David Burliuk Prize for life-long commitment to experimental poetry (2010).

Yuri Milorava was born in 1952 in Tbilisi, Georgia. A graduate of Tbilisi University for Foreign Languages, he lived in Moscow in the 1990s, later moved to Chicago, Illinois, and then returned to Moscow. From the 1980s his poems appeared in émigré Russian and Ukrainian periodicals, e.g. in *The Continent, Chernovik* and *Khreschatyk,* and later in *The Anthology of Russian Vers Libre* (1991). He has published three collections of his poems, *Instead* (1996), *Distaff Angel* (2003) and *Ovejo* (2016), as well as his memoir about Viktor Shklovsky. He has also translated French and Georgian poetry into Russian.

Sasha Moroz was born in 1990 in Moscow. She was educated at Russian State University for the Humanities, where she studied cultural anthropology, and now is doing postgraduate studies at the Institute of Philosophy, Russian Academy of Science and also studies contemporary art practices at Anatoly Osmolovsky's BAZA Institute. Her poems and literary translations appeared in Russian periodicals. Her debut collection is entitled *Nationality Square* (Free Poetry Publishing, 2020). In 2017, her poems made the long list of the Arkady Dragomoshchenko Prize.

Sergey Tenyatnikov was born in 1981 in Krasnoyarsk. He lived in Moscow and in Germany, and now is based on the Isle of Majorca, Spain. His poems appeared in both Russian and German literary periodicals. The debut collection of his German-language poems, *A Cuckoo Hatches from Your Eye (Aus deinem Auge schlüpft der Kuckuck)*, was published in Leipzig in 2017; the second book of his poems in German, *Plutarch's Head (Plutarchs Kopf)*, in Herford in 2019. His first collection of Russian poems entitled *Gutenberg Island* was published in Moscow, also in 2019. In 2014, he was the winner of the Emigrant Lyre Prize; in 2015, the recipient of the Astafyev Foundation literary award.

More poetry published by SurVision Books

Noelle Kocot. *Humanity*
(New Poetics: USA)
ISBN 978-1-9995903-0-7

Ciaran O'Driscoll. *The Speaking Trees*
(New Poetics: Ireland)
ISBN 978-1-9995903-1-4

Helen Ivory. *Maps of the Abandoned City*
(New Poetics: England)
ISBN 978-1-912963-04-1

Elin O'Hara Slavick. *Cameramouth*
(New Poetics: USA)
ISBN 978-1-9995903-4-5

John W. Sexton. *Inverted Night*
(New Poetics: Ireland)
ISBN 978-1-912963-05-8

Afric McGlinchey. *Invisible Insane*
(New Poetics: Ireland)
ISBN 978-1-9995903-3-8

Anatoly Kudryavitsky. *Stowaway*
(New Poetics: Ireland)
ISBN 978-1-9995903-2-1

Tim Murphy. *The Cacti Do Not Move*
(New Poetics: Ireland)
ISBN 978-1-912963-07-2

Tony Kitt. *The Magic Phlute*
  (New Poetics: Ireland)
  ISBN 978-1-912963-08-9

Clayre Benzadón. *Liminal Zenith*
  (New Poetics: USA)
  ISBN 978-1-912963-11-9

Thomas Townsley. *Tangent of Ardency*
  (New Poetics: USA)
  ISBN 978-1-912963-15-7

George Kalamaras. *That Moment of Wept*
  ISBN 978-1-9995903-7-6

Anton Yakovlev. *Chronos Dines Alone*
  (Winner of James Tate Poetry Prize 2018)
  ISBN 978-1-912963-01-0

Bob Lucky. *Conversation Starters in a Language No One Speaks*
  (Winner of James Tate Poetry Prize 2018)
  ISBN 978-1-912963-00-3

Christopher Prewitt. *Paradise Hammer*
  (Winner of James Tate Poetry Prize 2018)
  ISBN 978-1-9995903-9-0

Mikko Harvey & Jake Bauer. *Idaho Falls*
  (Winner of James Tate Poetry Prize 2018)
  ISBN 978-1-912963-02-7

Tony Bailie. *Mountain Under Heaven*
  (Winner of James Tate Poetry Prize 2019)
  ISBN 978-1-912963-09-6

Nicholas Alexander Hayes. *Amorphous Organics*
(Winner of James Tate Poetry Prize 2019)
ISBN 978-1-912963-10-2

John Bradley. *Spontaneous Mummification*
(Winner of James Tate Poetry Prize 2019)
ISBN 978-1-912963-13-3

John Thomas Allen. *Rolling in the Third Eye*
(Winner of James Tate Poetry Prize 2019)
ISBN 978-1-912963-15-7

Gary Glauber. *The Covalence of Equanimity*
(Winner of James Tate Poetry Prize 2019)
ISBN 978-1-912963-12-6

Maria Grazia Calandrone. *Fossils*
Translated from Italian
(New Poetics: Italy)
ISBN 978-1-9995903-6-9

Sergey Biryukov. *Transformations*
Translated from Russian
(New Poetics: Russia)
ISBN 978-1-9995903-5-2

Alexander Korotko. *Irrazionalismo*
Translated from Russian
(New Poetics: Ukraine)
ISBN 978-1-912963-06-5

Anton G. Leitner. *Selected Poems 1981–2015*
Translated from German
ISBN 978-1-9995903-8-3

All our books are available to order via
http://survisionmagazine.com/books.htm

www.ingramcontent.com/pod-product-compliance
Lightning Source LLC
LaVergne TN
LVHW021613080426
835510LV00019B/2553